Au revoir les enfants

Au revoir les enfants

A Screenplay by

LOUIS MALLE

TRANSLATED FROM THE FRENCH
by Anselm Hollo

GROVE PRESS
New York

Originally published in French, copyright © 1987 by Éditions Gallimard
English translation copyright © 1988 by Anselm Hollo

All photographs copyright © 1987 Orion Pictures Corporation

Published by Grove Press, Inc.
920 Broadway
New York, N.Y. 10010

Library of Congress Cataloging-in-Publication Data

Malle, Louis
  [Au revoir les enfants. English]
  Au revoir les enfants-Goodbye, children: a screenplay by Louis Malle; trans-
lated from the French by Anselm Hollo.—1st ed.
  p. cm.
  ISBN: 0–8021–3114–X (pbk.)
  1. World War, 1939–1945—Drama.   I. Au revoir les enfants.
II. Title.   III. Title: Goodbye, children.
PN1997.R53413M3   1988   87–34656
791.43′72—dc19   CIP

Designed by Irving Perkins Associates, Inc.
Manufactured in the United States of America
First Edition 1988
10 9 8 7 6 5 4 3 2 1

Preface

Au revoir les enfants is inspired by the most tragic memory of my childhood. In 1944, I was eleven years old and boarding at a Catholic school near Fontainebleau. A new boy joined us at the beginning of the year. A brilliant student, he intrigued me. He was different; his background was mysterious. He didn't talk much the first few weeks. Little by little we became friends, when, one morning, our small world collapsed.

That morning of 1944 changed my life. It may have triggered my becoming a filmmaker. I should have made it the subject of my first film, but I preferred to wait. Time passed, the memory became more acute. In 1986, after almost ten years in the United States, I felt the moment had come and wrote the script of *Au revoir les enfants*. Memory serving as a springboard for imagination, I reinvented the past in the pursuit of a haunting and timeless truth.

Through the eyes of Julien Quentin, a young boy with my background and temperament, I have tried to evoke this first friendship—brutally destroyed—and my discovery of the real world—its violence, it disorder, its prejudices. 1944 is far away, but I know that adolescents of today can share my emotions.

New York, 1987   LOUIS MALLE

Cast

JULIEN QUENTIN	Gaspard Manesse
JEAN BONNET	Raphaël Fejtö
MME QUENTIN	Francine Racette
FRANÇOIS QUENTIN	Stanislas Carré de Malberg
FATHER JEAN	Philippe Morier-Genoud
FATHER MICHEL	François Berléand
JOSEPH	François Négret
MULLER	Peter Fitz
BOULANGER	Pascal Rivet
CIRON	Benoit Henriet
SAGARD	Richard Leboeuf
BABINOT	Xavier Legrand
NÉGUS/ LAFARGE	Arnaud Henriet
LAVIRON	Jean-Sébastien Chauvin
MOREAU	Luc Étienne
M. TINCHAUT	Daniel Edinger
M. GUIBOURG	Marcel Bellot
M. FLORENT	Ami Flammer
MLLE DAVENNE	Irène Jacob
FATHER HIPPOLYTE	Jean-Paul Dubarry
INFIRMARY NURSE	Jacqueline Staup
MME PERRIN	Jacqueline Paris

And

René Bouloc, Alain Clément, Michaël Rottstock, Detlef Gericke, Michaël Becker, Thomas Friedl, Christian Sohn, Michel Ginot, Philippe Despaux

Credits

Writer/Producer/Director	Louis Malle
Associate Producer	Christian Ferry
Cinematography	Renato Berta
Art Direction	Willy Holt
Costume Designer	Corinne Jorry
Sound	Jean-Claude Laureux
Editor	Émmanuelle Castro
Assistant Editor	Marie-France Poulizac
Continuity	France La Chapelle
Makeup/Hairdresser	Susan Robertson
Assistant Director	Yann Gilbert
Sound Mix	Claude Villand
Sound Effects	Daniel Couteau
Production Manager	Gérald Molto
Assistant Production Manager	Jean-Yves Asselin
Casting	Jeanne Biras, Iris Carrière
Music	*Moment musical no. 2*, by Schubert
	Rondo Capriccioso, by Saint-Saëns
	Ami Flammer, *violin*
	J. F. Heisser, *piano*

Au revoir les enfants is a French-German Co-production
NOUVELLES ÉDITIONS DE FILMS S.A., Paris
M.K.2. PRODUCTIONS, Paris
STELLA FILM GmbH, Munich
N.E.F. GmbH, Munich

Au revoir les enfants

1

Gare de Lyon, January 3, 1944. A forty-year-old woman and a twelve-year-old boy are standing in front of a wooden railroad car, the kind in which every compartment has its own door. They stand facing each other, motionless in the flow of travelers. He is wearing short pants, a navy-blue sweater, and a black cape. She is wearing an elaborate hat and a knee-length "austerity" fur coat. It is obvious that she has applied her makeup too hastily: one cheek is redder than the other; her lipstick spreads over the contours of her lips.

THE MOTHER: Julien, you promised.

JULIEN (*hanging his head*): I'm not crying. I'm not crying at all.

THE MOTHER: I'll come visit you in three weeks. And then you'll have your vacation for Mardi Gras. You'll see, time will go really fast.

(JULIEN *raises his head. His eyes are glistening.*)

JULIEN: Why do you say that? You know very well that it won't go fast.

THE MOTHER: Your father and I will write to you often.

JULIEN: I don't give a damn for Papa. I hate you.

(*Behind them, two boys with knapsacks climb the steps of the car.*)

3

THE BOYS: Hello, Quentin . . . How are you, madam . . .

THE MOTHER: Hello, hello . . . Well, I'm sure you're glad to
see your schoolmates again.

JULIEN: Sure, like Sagard! What a cretin. I can't stand him.

(*She laughs. He throws himself at her and clings to her, forlorn. A
whistle, last calls. The stationmaster waves his flag. A sixteen-year-
old boy joins them.*)

THE BOY: Hey, still smooching. My dear Julien, surely you
don't want to miss the train, being such a model student
and all.

(*He takes one last drag on his cigarette and tosses the butt.*)

THE MOTHER: François, you're not allowed to smoke.

FRANÇOIS: That isn't tobacco, it's corn silk. That doesn't
count . . . Goodbye, Mama. Take care.

(*He kisses his MOTHER and joins a friend who is waiting for him.
THE MOTHER kneels in front of JULIEN and kisses him on the
cheek. Her lipstick leaves a visible oval trace.*)

THE MOTHER: All right, get on now.

(*She leads him toward the compartment door but he turns and presses
himself against her as hard as he can, his arms around her neck, his
nose in her corsage. She whispers, stroking the back of his neck.*)

THE MOTHER: And me? You don't think about me? You
think I'm happy about this? I miss you every moment. I
would love to disguise myself as a boy and come to school
with you. Then I could see you every day. That would be
our secret . . .

(*THE MOTHER's voice is drowned out by the whistle of a moving
train.*)

2

The train window is frosted over. A gust of black coal-smoke darkens the image for a moment. The locomotive can be heard straining. JULIEN *watches the winter landscape moving past. Behind him, three boys his own age are fighting, climbing onto the seats, hanging from the luggage racks like monkeys. In the window reflection,* JULIEN *sees the trace of lipstick on his cheek. He wipes it off, mechanically, with the back of his sleeve. His expression has softened. He is weeping.*

3

The old part of a small town in Île-de-France. Forty-odd boys are proceeding up the street in loose formation, singing a Boy Scout song. All of them are dressed exactly like JULIEN. *The knapsacks look like humps under their capes. The wooden soles of their shoes clack against the ground. Two German soldiers, off duty, stop to watch them pass. A young monk in a maroon-colored frock, corpulent and friendly, is walking and singing along with the boys.* FATHER MICHEL, *whom the students among themselves call "Mother Michel," is wearing sandals on his bare feet.*

FATHER MICHEL: Hello, Julien. Did you have a good vacation?

JULIEN (*scowling*): Yes, Father.

FATHER MICHEL: Your parents are well?

JULIEN: Yes, Father.

(*The boy next to* JULIEN, BABINOT, *speaks with a lisp.*)

BABINOT: What did they give you for Christmas?

JULIEN: Books.

BABINOT: Books? Nothing else?

JULIEN: Just books.

BABINOT: How weird.

(*The boys pass through a large gateway into a courtyard. There is a plaque: Carmelite Convent. School of Saint John of the Cross.*)

4

The boys' dormitory is a converted chapel. Each student has a locker in the big cupboards by the walls to keep his things in. There are thirty beds in the dormitory. In a corner stands a wooden bed, which belongs to MOREAU, *a young supervisor without any real authority. The students poke fun at him, but find him* simpàtico. JULIEN, *in his pajamas, pulls jars of preserves and a kilogram of sugar out of his pack. He is about to put them into his locker when* CIRON, *a tall beanpole of a boy, grabs one of the preserve jars.*

CIRON (*in a mock German accent*): Ach. Ze black market, m'sieu Quentin. Ve haf to arrest you. Ze prezerves, ve confiscate.

(JULIEN *chases him, knocks him onto a bed, and retrieves his property. He walks past some boys—two of whom are twins—standing around a big wood-burning stove, the only heat in the dormitory. They're looking at a photograph and whispering.* JULIEN *takes the photo and looks at it.*)

JULIEN: She doesn't even have tits.

A VOICE (*by the door*): Watch out! *Babasses!*

("Babasses" *refers to monks in the argot of their school.* FATHER JEAN, *head of the school, a man of forty with the face of an ascetic, and* FATHER HIPPOLYTE *enter the dormitory accompanied by three boys who aren't wearing the school uniform. The youngest of these boys is wearing a beige coat that is too small for him.* FATHER JEAN *leads him to the bed next to* JULIEN'S. *All the students greet him with a respectful* "Bonjour, mon Père.")

FATHER JEAN: This bed is free?

MOREAU: Yes, Father. Ever since d'Éparville got the whooping cough.

FATHER JEAN: So, this is yours then, my little friend. Children, this is Jean Bonnet, your new classmate.

(*Surprising everybody, he bends down to kiss* BONNET'S *forehead.*)

FATHER JEAN: Monsieur Moreau, please find a locker for him. Good night, children.

THE STUDENTS: Good night, Father.

(*At the door,* FATHER JEAN *rejoins the two older new boys and* FATHER HIPPOLYTE. *As soon as they have left,* BONNET *is hit in the face by a pillow followed by several others. At the same time, all kinds of jokes based on the newcomer's name are heard:* "Night bonnet, donkey's bonnet. . . .")

MOREAU: Leave him alone and get ready for bed.

(*He leads* BONNET *to an empty locker. The students undress, put on pajamas or nightshirts.* BONNET *unpacks his things. He takes out several books and puts them on his bed. As he turns around, he sees* JULIEN, *who is watching him.*)

BONNET: What's your name?

(JULIEN *does not reply. He picks up one of* BONNET'S *books.*)

JULIEN (*reads*): "The Adventures of Sherlock Holmes." (*He pronounces it* "Holmesse.")

(*All of a sudden, the lights go out. Shouts, laughter.*)

MOREAU: That's just a brownout. Get into your beds.

(JULIEN *and several other students have flashlights. A boy points his flashlight at his chin, making his face seem lit from within. He jumps up and down, uttering raucous cries.* JULIEN *moves quite close to* BONNET, *face to face.*)

JULIEN: My name is Julien Quentin, and you can find me if you look for me.

(*Everybody settles in for the night.* BONNET, *still fully dressed, gazes at the tall statue of the Virgin that stands against the wall he is facing.* JULIEN *picks up a book from the night table, dives under the covers with his flashlight, and starts looking for his page.*)

5

Morning. The students go through the motions of washing. They hardly wet their heads, but shake themselves, hop on one leg, then the other. BONNET *notices that a stalactite of frozen water protrudes from a faucet of his washbasin under a window. He breaks the icicle off and gently places it on the windowsill. He turns on the other faucet. For a few seconds, nothing happens, but then a jet of freezing water strikes him. He jumps back, utters a cry.*

BONNET: There's no hot water?

BOULANGER: No, there's no hot water. We're not sissies here.

(BOULANGER, *a very corpulent boy, picks up the icicle and slips it behind* BONNET'S *shirt collar.*)

6

All the students of the school are in the pews of the chapel listening to
FATHER JEAN, *who is standing at the altar wearing celebrant's
vestments and reading the Gospel. There are a few monks in the
wooden stalls.* BOULANGER *seems ill at ease. He raises his hand to his
face, several times.*

VOICE OF FATHER JEAN: Truly, truly, I say unto you, unless
you eat the flesh of the Son of Man and drink his blood,
you will have no life in you.

(*Suddenly,* BOULANGER *sways and keels over backwards in a faint,
a truly spectacular fall.* MOREAU *rushes over and with the help of a
young monk picks him up and carries him out of the chapel. They pass
in front of* BONNET, *who is sitting in the last row in the company of
a big boy with curly hair and a redhead. The three newcomers.*
FRANÇOIS, *sitting next to* JULIEN, *comments.*)

FRANÇOIS: There's nothing to eat, we're freezing to death, but
we can't have breakfast before communion. What a
place . . .

JULIEN: Are you going to take communion?

FRANÇOIS: I'm not an ass-kisser like you.

(FATHER JEAN *has resumed, as if the incident were routine.*)

FATHER JEAN: He who eats my flesh and drinks my blood has
eternal life and I will raise him up at the last day. For my
flesh is food indeed and my blood is drink indeed. He
who eats my flesh and drinks my blood abides in me, and
I in him.

(*A single clap of hands. The students kneel and intone the offertory
chant.* JULIEN *rocks from one knee to the other, pain showing in his
face.*)

FRANÇOIS: What's wrong?

JULIEN: I've got frostbite on my knees.

FRANÇOIS (*peremptorily*): What you need is a shot of calvados.

7

The seventh-grade class. There are fifteen students. Several among them, including JULIEN, *are wearing wool gloves even while writing.* M. TINCHAUT *is striding back and forth, his coat slung over his shoulders.* JULIEN, *standing by his desk, is reading out loud, fast and very poorly.*

JULIEN: "Star of the sea, Here lies the heavy sheet
        And the deep swell and the ocean of wheat
        And the turbulent spume and our full granaries,
        Here, your eyes on this immense cope,
        And here your voice on this weighty plain
        Our absent friends, depopulated hearts,
        Here, the stretch of our shattered fists
        And our weariness, and our full force.
        Morning star, inaccessible Queen . . ."

M. TINCHAUT: Quentin, you're ready for the Comédie Française. Could you remind us who Charles Péguy was?

JULIEN: He was killed in the war of 1914.

M. TINCHAUT: Good. But you're starting at the end.

JULIEN: His mother was a chair mender.

(*Some laughter.*)

M. TINCHAUT: No cause for stupid guffaws. Péguy's mother was a woman of great merit.

(*He approaches* BONNET.)

M. TINCHAUT: Monsieur Bonnot, do you know anything about Charles Péguy?

BONNET: No, sir. My name is Bonnet.

BABINOT: As in Dubo, Dubon, Dubonnet.

(*All the others join in the chorus.*)

M. TINCHAUT: Very witty, Babinot. Now, so you'll get back into the flow of things after your vacation, you will write a commentary on the first two stanzas of the poem. You have half an hour.

(*The students get to work.* JULIEN *writes a couple of lines, then stops. Head raised, he daydreams for a moment. His eyes turn to* BONNET, *who is writing rapidly with great concentration and keeps raising his left hand to his ear. A voice is heard from outside.* BONNET *looks up.* JULIEN *follows his gaze. In the courtyard, a very young German soldier, bareheaded, stands talking to a monk.* BONNET *returns to his writing.* JULIEN *picks up his compass. He pricks the back of his hand with the sharp point several times until it starts bleeding.*)

BOULANGER (*who sits next to him*): You're crazy.

JULIEN: It doesn't even hurt.

(BONNET *is looking at him.*)

8

The students, big and small, at recess in the schoolyard. Several boys are kicking their heels against the wall, talking. Others are working on the horizontal bar under the supervision of the gymnastics teacher. In the middle of the yard, twenty-odd students of all ages are walking on stilts and trying to knock each other over. Theoretically, there are two teams, but the game soon deteriorates into separate duels. It is

quite brutal: falls onto the frozen ground are painful. FATHER
MICHEL *is playing with the boys, trying to keep order, but he has
trouble with his stilts, and* JULIEN *knocks him down.*

FATHER MICHEL: Easy, Quentin, easy.

(*Hidden from view by a woodpile,* FRANÇOIS *and another big boy,*
PESSOZ, *are sharing a cigarette.* BONNET *is reading, leaning
against the wall. Five boys from the seventh grade come up from
behind and grab him. Two take hold of his legs, another two grab his
arms, and the fifth pushes down on his stomach: thus they inflict upon
him the "bone-shaker," a hazing ritual.* BONNET *squirms like an
earthworm.* JULIEN *makes a quick turn around an adversary, feints,
charges, trips the other's stilts. His opponent crashes down.* JULIEN,
*uttering shouts of triumph, raises one stilt in the air and jumps
around on one leg.*)

JULIEN: Notre Dame! *Montjoie!* I am Bayard, *le Chevalier sans
    peur et sans reproche.*

A BIG BOY: So, little Quentin, we're a real terror, are we?

(*He charges* JULIEN *and slams into him with his shoulder.* JULIEN,
*still balancing on only one stilt, loses his balance and takes a bad fall.
He stays on the ground, holding his battered knee. His face is puckered
up, but he restrains himself and does not cry.*)

JULIEN: Laviron, you bastard.

(*A boy challenges* LAVIRON. *He is a sturdy fourteen-year-old with
black frizzy hair whom we have seen sitting next to* BONNET *at
Mass.*)

THE BOY: Come on, you laggard, traitor, knave. This is me,
    Négus, the Black Knight, protector of the orphans and
    the weak.

(*Cries are heard: "Go, Négus," "Go, Laviron." A big circle forms,
and the fight becomes a parody of a medieval joust.*)

LAVIRON: Stand back, you wog. I am Richard Coeur de Lion, the pride of Christendom. I'll boot you out of Jerusalem, infidel Saracen, son of a bitch.

NÉGUS (*adopting a fake Arabic accent*): Allah iss God, and Mahomet iss his prophet. You are trambling my frand. Lion heart, bone head, chicken shit, horse's ass . . .

(*He circles around* LAVIRON *and then charges him, yelling.*)

NÉGUS: Allah, Allah, Allah, Allah . . .

(*The antics of* NÉGUS *amuse the spectators, who keep encouraging both combatants.* JULIEN *has gotten up.* BONNET *stands behind him.*)

BONNET: Go, Négus!

JULIEN: That's his real name, Négus?

BONNET: What do you think?

JULIEN (*irritated*): Is he ever ugly. You know him?

BONNET: His name's Lafarge, and he's my best friend.

(NÉGUS, *less steady on his stilts, gets tripped and falls. He gets up immediately, holding a stilt in front of him like a lance.* FATHER MICHEL's *whistle signals the end of recess. Reluctantly, the students disperse.*)

FATHER MICHEL: Babinot, hurry up.

9

JULIEN *is sitting on the big kitchen table.* MME PERRIN, *a large maternal woman fond of her wine, is washing his knee and applying vinegar to the abrasion.* JULIEN *lets out a yell.*

MME PERRIN (*who has a northern French accent*): That doesn't hurt one bit. Now hold still, and I'll put a bandage on it. You're going to kill yourself with those stilts. Those are games fit only for savages. One of these days there will be a broken leg . . .

(JULIEN *is not listening. He is watching* JOSEPH, *the kitchen worker, who is quietly negotiating with one of the big boys. The latter hands him a box of candy, picks a bank note from his fingers, and exits running.* JOSEPH, *who has a limp, runs after him.*)

JOSEPH: Hey, not enough! We said forty-five.

MME PERRIN: Joseph, what tricks are you up to again? Get back to your potatoes.

(JOSEPH *comes back into the kitchen, slips the candy into his apron pocket.*)

JOSEPH: The richer they are, the more they steal.

(JOSEPH *is seventeen years old, sickly, with one leg shorter than the other. He has the demeanor and vocabulary of a cocky Parisian kid, impudent and never at a loss for words. He is also a constant whistler. He returns to his cutting board. The cook helps herself to a large glass of red wine.*)

JOSEPH: Madame Perrin, you're drinking too much.

MME PERRIN: Shut up, you little jerk. There's nothing wrong with a little drop of what's good for you.

(JULIEN *goes over to* JOSEPH *and whispers.*)

JULIEN: You got any stamps?

JOSEPH: I won't do any more business with you guys.

JULIEN: I've got some preserves.

(JOSEPH *casts a glance at* MME PERRIN.)

JOSEPH: After lunch, okay? The doctor's wife, she's crazy

about your jam. It gives her ovaries a boost, you know what I mean?

10

The refectory. Six student tables are arranged in two rows. Monks, teachers, and supervisors sit at a very long table alongside the wall. JULIEN *is sitting with the boys of his class, close to the kitchen.* BONNET *is at the end of the table. A plate of meat is passed from hand to hand.*

SAGARD: Now there's straw in the bread. I'm going to write to my father.

BOULANGER: Pass the basket.

(*There is a basket at the end of each table which contains students' personal provisions.* BOULANGER *picks from it a large tin on which his name is inscribed in large characters. It contains butter and potted meat.* FATHER JEAN, *who is eating with a hearty appetite, raises his eyes, then rings the bell.*)

FATHER JEAN: I would like to remind those who have personal provisions to share them with their fellow students.

BABINOT (*lisping*) : I've got some sardines, but I don't have a key for the tin. Anyone have a key?

ROLLIN: Who would like some sausage? I have to tell you, it's horsemeat.

(BOULANGER *finishes spreading the potted meat on his piece of bread, closes the tin, and returns it to the basket.*)

BOULANGER: I have to eat that stuff. I'm anemic.

CIRON: And what about us? Did you hear what Father Jean said?

BOULANGER (*with his mouth full*): There isn't enough for everybody. Your parents will just have to take care of you.

(*The meat plate reaches* NAVARRE, *who sits next to* BONNET.)

NAVARRE: There's only one slice left.

BONNET: Help yourself.

NAVARRE: Thank you. You're a sport.

(*The bell rings again. One of the students goes to stand in the middle of the refectory and reads, in relative silence.*)

THE STUDENT: Today, Saint Simeon the Stylite. "Saint Simeon the Stylite was thirteen years old, herding his father's sheep, when he heard this verse from the Gospel: 'Woe unto you who are laughing now, for the day shall come when you shall weep.' He left his parents, became a hermit, and lived for thirty years on top of a column." (*Laughter.*) "He stayed there without shade or shelter, absorbed in practically continuous prayer . . ."

(*The reading ends in the midst of laughter and chatter.* JULIEN *stands on his bench and assumes the pose of a statue. The meal is over. The students begin to leave.* BONNET *is eating his apple, his eyes somewhere else.*)

MOREAU (*to everybody*): Vitamin crackers. Vitamin crackers.

(*He goes from one table to the next, carrying a large box. Every student receives a cracker.* JULIEN *stretches out one hand behind his shoulder, then the other.* MOREAU, *distracted, gives him two crackers.* BONNET *lets* SAGARD *take his cracker.* SAGARD *puts it into his mouth, licks it, then hands it back.*)

SAGARD: Here. It's better now.

(BONNET *pushes* SAGARD *aside and gets up to leave the table.* JULIEN *offers him a cracker.*)

JULIEN: I got two of them.

BONNET: Thank you. I'm not hungry anymore.

(*He moves off.*)

JULIEN: He gets on my nerves, that guy.

(JOSEPH, *who is sweeping up peelings, leans down to* JULIEN.)

JOSEPH: You have the preserves?

(JULIEN *nods.* FRANÇOIS *and some of his buddies pass by.* PESSOZ *grabs* JOSEPH'S *arm, twists it, and forces him to the floor.*)

JOSEPH: Stop. These are my clean pants.

(JOSEPH'S *wallet falls to the ground, and a photograph drops out.* PESSOZ *picks it up and waves it about.*)

PESSOZ: Hey, boys, Joseph is in love.

(JOSEPH *wrests the photograph from him.*)

PESSOZ: She looks like a slut, your fiancée.

JOSEPH: And your sister? What does your sister look like?

(*He limps off at a run, pursued by* PESSOZ. *It is obvious that he is the students' whipping boy.* JULIEN *takes his jar of preserves and runs after* JOSEPH.)

11

JULIEN *rejoins* JOSEPH *in a small poultry yard where three young pigs are kept in a makeshift wire enclosure.* JOSEPH *throws the peelings to the pigs, who start fighting for them.*

JOSEPH: In a month, they'll be ready to eat.

JULIEN: Fat chance! They'll keep those for the big school party, so our parents can say, "My, but the food is wonderful here!" Let's see your stamps.

(JOSEPH *takes an envelope from his pocket.*)

JOSEPH: There's a fifteen centimes Madagascar in here. The guy said it's very rare.

JULIEN: *Pretty* rare.

(JULIEN *takes a look at the contents of the envelope and returns it to him.*)

JULIEN: Not too bad. But I think I'll keep my preserves. The food is so disgusting here.

JOSEPH: You really are a Jew, aren't you.

(*He pulls another envelope out of his pocket.* JULIEN *gives him the jar of preserves and pockets both envelopes.*)

JULIEN: So, you're in love?

JOSEPH: No joke, it's serious. You wouldn't have a spare fifty I could borrow? You know, women are such an expensive business! You'll find out.

JULIEN: No, I won't. And besides, you're rolling in it.

JOSEPH: Sure, with all the money they're paying me . . . If only I could find another job . . .

JULIEN (*walking away*): I just don't have the cash. Ask François.

12

M. GUIBOURG, *the mathematics teacher, is at the blackboard. He is wearing his sheepskin jacket, his beret, and gloves.*

M. GUIBOURG: Ciron, put some more wood in the stove. It's freezing in here.

(CIRON *gets up and clicks his heels with a military salute.*)

M. GUIBOURG (*without turning to look*): And don't feel obliged to play the fool . . . Who can show me that in this quadrilateral the sum of the two opposite sides AB plus CD equals the sum of the other two, BC plus DA?

(*Several hands are raised, including* BONNET's.)

M. GUIBOURG: You—the new boy.

CIRON: Sir, his name is Dubonnet.

BONNET: That's all right.

(BONNET *goes to the blackboard. Another student stretches out a leg and trips him. Laughter.*)

BONNET: We know that tangents to a circle, coming from the same point, are equal. Therefore, a equals a, b equals b.

(*He solves the problem with ease.*)

M. GUIBOURG: That's very good. Has everybody understood?

THE STUDENTS: Yes, sir!

(*A distant siren is heard, then another one, very close.*)

A VOICE: Great, an air raid.

(*The students start getting up, delighted with this diversion.*)

M. GUIBOURG: We're going down to the shelter. But class isn't over. Bring your books.

13

The cellar of the school. The seventh-graders are packed tight on benches in a long passage extending back into darkness. Pipes run along the walls. A little light is given off by a bulb on the ceiling. A *doorway leads to a room partly filled with empty boxes, where another group of students is accommodated. They can be heard but not seen. * FATHER MICHEL *tries to create order. He is holding a hurricane lamp.*

A VOICE (*singing*): Mother Michel has lost her cat . . .

FATHER MICHEL: Silence! Boulanger, make room. Monsieur Guibourg, you come over here.

(*He pushes a chair over to* M. GUIBOURG, *who sits down and starts to read in the light provided by the father's lamp.*)

M. GUIBOURG: Lesson number fifteen, page 52. The product of two powers of the same decimal relative to . . .

(JULIEN *produces his flashlight and points it at his book.*)

BONNET: May I share that?

(*He brings his book closer to* JULIEN'S. *The latter, however, is not following the class text. His book is* The Three Musketeers.)

BONNET: Hold your flashlight a little higher. I can't see.

JULIEN: Leave me alone. You'll get me into trouble. And you piss me off.

(*He turns away. Rumbling sounds are heard, and the ceiling light goes out.* M. GUIBOURG *stops reading. The boys are restless in the near-dark.*)

A VOICE: They're bombing the railroad station.

ANOTHER VOICE: No, that's not it! That's the artillery barracks.

FATHER MICHEL: Calm down. Sit down.

(*He starts reciting a Hail Mary.* JULIEN *prays with the others. Without thinking he rotates the beam of his flashlight around him. Bodies and faces are lit briefly and vanish again. Then the beam stops on two boys entwined in each other's arms. Startled by the light, they separate.)*

A STUDENT: Lovebirds! (*Laughter.*)

FATHER MICHEL: Quentin, switch that off.

14

In the dormitory, the kneeling students are finishing their evening prayers. BONNET *gets up without making the sign of the cross and slides between the sheets. Several times, he tries to stretch out his legs —in vain. All the others are watching this. There are outbursts of laughter.*

LAVIRON: You'll just have to curl up like a little doggie!

(BONNET *raises the covers and sees that his bed has been short-sheeted. He turns to* JULIEN.)

BONNET: Did you do this?

(JULIEN *stares at him without answering and goes to bed. Later that night,* JULIEN *seems to be having a lovely dream. He smiles, turns over on his side. His lips move; he sighs. Then the smile is extinguished, becomes a grimace. He opens his eyes, sits up, and slides his hand under the covers. He looks left and right: everybody is asleep. He gets out of bed, unfolds the covers. There is a large damp stain in the middle of the sheet.)*

JULIEN: Shit, shit, shit, shit, shit.

(*He gets a towel from the end of the bed and starts scrubbing like mad, trying to dry the sheet. He is shivering. He moves the sheet as far down toward the end of the bed as possible, places the towel on top of the stain, and gets back into bed again. He lies there with his eyes open, still shivering, trying to find a position in which his body won't come into contact with the damp part of the sheet. He hears someone cry out: "No! No! No!" A few beds away, a boy sits up, his back hunched, and strikes out with his fists into the void, as if he were defending himself against the Invisible Man.* BONNET *wakes up suddenly.*)

BONNET: What! What is it?

(*He sees* JULIEN, *who is looking at him, calms down, settles down again.*)

15

The seventh-graders are doing gymnastics in the schoolyard. JULIEN *follows* CIRON *on the horizontal bar. He tries a flip and doesn't manage it. The others are doing push-ups on the ground, goaded by the teacher, a retired noncommissioned officer. Several are wearing ski masks. One after another they collapse on the ground.*

THE TEACHER: Knees straight, shoulders back! Your biceps must be *papier-mâché*.

(*An attractive girl enters the yard on a man's bicycle. A large cardboard portfolio, attached to the handlebars, impedes her balance. She rides past the boys with a smile for the teacher who follows her with his eyes, forgetting his charges. As she dismounts, she stumbles but does not fall; there is a glimpse of her thighs. All the boys are watching her.*)

BOULANGER: She did that on purpose. To flash her ass at us.

CIRON: She's got a nicer ass than you do.

THE TEACHER: Silence! Ciron, give me another twenty push-ups.

(*The girl walks toward the music room.* FRANÇOIS *and* PESSOZ *appear and engage her in conversation.*)

16

The music room. JULIEN *is playing Schubert's* Moment musical *no. 2, very slowly, very poorly. The young woman seen on the bicycle,* MLLE DAVENNE, *is sitting just behind the piano. She is doing her nails.* JULIEN *looks at her breasts, and this leads him to make a serious fingering mistake.*

MLLE DAVENNE (*without raising her head*): That's a sharp. You don't hear a wrong note when you hit one?

(JULIEN *starts over, reluctantly.* MLLE DAVENNE *yawns.*)

MLLE DAVENNE: You should try the violin.

(JULIEN *laughs. They both laugh.*)

MLLE DAVENNE: You hate music, is that it?

JULIEN: Not at all. It's my mother who forces me to take piano.

MLLE DAVENNE: She's right to do that. If you stop now, you'll regret it all your life. Well, time's up. See you Tuesday!

(*The door opens.* BONNET *enters. He passes* JULIEN *and awkwardly proceeds to the piano.*)

MLLE DAVENNE: What's your name?

BONNET: Jean Bonnet.

MLLE DAVENNE: Well, let's hear you play.

(JULIEN *leaves. Outside, he can hear the first notes of his piece. He turns back, presses his nose against the glass-paned door.* MLLE DAVENNE *is smiling.* BONNET *executes the Schubert piece with ease. Tempo and pitch are correct.*)

MLLE DAVENNE: My goodness, you're really doing well. It's a
    pleasure to have a talented student.

(*Outside the door,* JULIEN *is shivering. He wraps his muffler around
his neck.*)

JULIEN: What an ass-kisser!

(*But he stays until* BONNET *has finished the piece.*)

17

*Before dinner, the students in the seventh-grade classroom are doing
their assignments.* FATHER HIPPOLYTE, *standing close to the stove,
his back turned, is telling his rosary beads.* JULIEN *is sorting his new
stamps.* BOULANGER *nudges him and nods in the direction of*
SAGARD *in the back of the room, who has the top of his desk raised
and whose face is tense.* BOULANGER *makes a pumping movement
with his hand.*

JULIEN (*whispers*): You think?

BOULANGER (*with conviction*): They say it turns you into an
    idiot. But with him, that's no risk.

(JULIEN *looks at* BONNET, *who is turning a piece of paper in his
hands, his gaze elsewhere. Then the boy next to him suddenly rips it
out of his hands.* BONNET *tries to get it back, but the boy passes it
behind his back.* BONNET *gets up and runs after the piece of paper,
which is passing from hand to hand.*)

FATHER HIPPOLYTE: Bonnet, go back to your desk.

(BONNET *sits down again but does not take his eyes off the piece of
paper, which gets to* JULIEN. *It is dog-eared and creased as if it had
been kept in a wallet for a long time.* JULIEN *unfolds it and sees the
writing in a large feminine hand with accented downstrokes.*)

JULIEN (*reading*): "My little darling, as you'll understand, it is very hard for me to write to you. Monsieur D. is going to Lyon and has offered to mail this letter. Your aunt and I are going out as little as possible . . ."

(*A student enters and speaks to* FATHER HIPPOLYTE.)

FATHER HIPPOLYTE: Julien Quentin, time to go to confession.

(JULIEN *gets up. He goes out of his way in order to pass* BONNET *and drops the letter on his desk.*)

JULIEN: Your mother's up to something.

18

FATHER JEAN'S *office.* JULIEN *is kneeling in the semidark, in the middle of the room. Sitting in front of him, a stole around his neck,* FATHER JEAN *is winding up the confession.*

JULIEN: Oh yes, I fought with my sister when I was on vacation.

FATHER JEAN: Are you sure you're not forgetting anything?

JULIEN: I don't think so.

FATHER JEAN: You haven't had any bad thoughts?

(JULIEN *looks at him.*)

FATHER JEAN: You know very well what I mean. Everybody has bad thoughts.

JULIEN: Even you?

(FATHER JEAN *smiles.*)

FATHER JEAN: Even me.

(JULIEN *wobbles from one knee to the other, making faces.*)

FATHER JEAN: What's the problem?

JULIEN: Frostbite.

FATHER JEAN: Let's see.

(JULIEN *gets up and shows him his knee.*)

FATHER JEAN: That's a vitamin deficiency. Tell Madame Perrin to give you some cod-liver oil.

JULIEN: It's really the cold. It's freezing here at school.

FATHER JEAN: I know. But remember those who are less fortunate than you. You told your mother that you would like to take holy orders.

JULIEN (*surprised*): She told you that?

(FATHER JEAN *nods.*)

FATHER JEAN: In my opinion, you have no vocation at all for holy orders.

JULIEN: You don't think I do?

FATHER JEAN: No, I'm sure you don't. And it's a sorry job, anyway.

(*He gives* JULIEN *absolution. We hear the strident ringing of a telephone.* JULIEN *is startled.* FATHER JEAN *gets up.*)

FATHER JEAN: Say three Hail Marys. You may stand.

(*He picks up the phone.* JULIEN *hears an excited, garbled voice at the other end of the line. We can make out a few words:* "*Attention . . . marked . . . precautions. . . .*")

FATHER JEAN: Where did you hear that? . . . Disregard rumors . . . What do you want me to do . . . We are in the Lord's hands.

(*He hangs up and remains lost in thought for a moment as if he had forgotten* JULIEN, *who is finishing his Hail Marys, his eyes on him all the while.*)

FATHER JEAN: Are you getting along all right with your new classmate?

JULIEN: Bonnet?

FATHER JEAN: Make sure to be kind to him. You have influence over the others. I'm counting on you.

JULIEN: But why? Is he sick?

FATHER JEAN: Oh no, not at all. All right, get along . . .

(JULIEN *leaves the room.* FATHER JEAN *looks after him with a little smile.*)

19

A square in the little town. Led by FATHER MICHEL, *the sixth- and seventh-graders are trudging through a dense fog in double ranks, carrying towels under their arms.* JULIEN *is reading* The Three Musketeers, *while walking along. Behind him,* BABINOT, SAGARD, *and* BOULANGER *are discussing politics.*

BABINOT: If we didn't have Pétain, we'd be in really deep shit.

BOULANGER: Who says that?

BABINOT: My father.

BOULANGER: Well, my father says that Laval has sold himself to the Germans.

SAGARD (*sententiously*): The Jews and the Communists are more dangerous than the Germans.

CIRON (*turning*): Your dad says that?

SAGARD: No, I say that.

(*A drunk on a bicycle zigzags past them. Laughter, breaking of ranks, jostling.*)

THE DRUNK (*at the top of his voice*): "Sweet Madelon, come bring us our drinks . . ."

(BONNET *is now walking next to* JULIEN. *The latter hides his book under his cape when* FATHER MICHEL *catches up with them.*)

BONNET: Good, isn't it?

JULIEN: What is?

BONNET: *The Three Musketeers.* How far have you got?

JULIEN: Where they're sitting in judgment of Milady.

BONNET: What a slut she is!

(JULIEN *gives him a cold stare.*)

JULIEN: What are you going to do later on?

BONNET: I don't know. Work on my math.

JULIEN: Math is such shit. What's the use of it, except if you want to become a bookkeeper.

BONNET: My father was a bookkeeper.

(*They turn into a side street and enter a public bathhouse, an ancient-looking establishment. A French policeman is standing in front of the door, on which a large sign is posted: This establishment is prohibited to Jews.*)

20

There are people in the dressing rooms of the baths. Some German soldiers are busy getting dressed, horsing around, and talking in loud voices. The students remain standing, intimidated, except for BONNET, *who sits down between two Germans and starts unlacing his shoes. A soldier strokes his cheek and says to his buddies, in German: "So fresh, so sweet." Loud laughter. The Germans leave. The students undress. Under the bench,* BABINOT *finds a magazine with photographs of naked women. He hides it under his clothes. Little* DU VALLIER *sits down next to* BONNET.

DU VALLIER: Bonnet, is it true that you don't take communion? Why don't you?

BONNET: I'm a Protestant.

(BOULANGER *shrinks back, holds his nose.*)

BOULANGER: A Huguenot! How disgusting.

(JULIEN *is unlacing his shoes next to* BONNET.)

JULIEN: That's not a Protestant name, Bonnet.

BONNET: It sure is.

(FATHER MICHEL, *in underpants, his torso bare, is ordering the students into the various showers of the public hall. There are also a few smaller rooms with bathtubs.*)

FATHER MICHEL: Ciron, here. . . Babinot, what do you think you're doing? . . . Bonnet, you take this tub.

ROLLIN: Can I have a tub, too?

FATHER MICHEL: All right, this one here.

ROLLIN: Oh no! It's too small, that tub. I can't get my legs into it.

FATHER MICHEL: You'll manage.

(*Later.* JULIEN *is daydreaming in his tub, immersed up to his neck. He has his hands underwater and is gently caressing himself. A piano is heard—the Schubert piece—and the voice of* MLLE DAVENNE: *"You should try the violin." There is a knock on the door.*)

FATHER MICHEL'S VOICE: Hurry up, Quentin. I'm waiting for your tub.

(JULIEN *wets his hair and rubs his ersatz soap into it. Then he immerses his head in the water. The door of the room opens.* FATHER MICHEL *enters, thinks the tub is empty, takes a step forward, and sees* JULIEN *underwater, motionless. He rushes up and pulls him out by his shoulders.* JULIEN *bursts out laughing.*)

FATHER MICHEL: What a smart aleck! I told you to hurry up . . .

(JULIEN *stands up in the tub, facing* FATHER MICHEL, *who turns his eyes away in embarrassment.*)

JULIEN: It's not my fault. My soap won't lather.

21

An icy wind has risen. The students are coming out of the baths, pulling their berets over their wet heads and beating their chests.

BOULANGER: Hurry up, we're freezing.

(*Behind them, a young man comes out of the baths. He is wearing only a jacket, but after a few steps he puts on his overcoat. The coat has a yellow star. He walks away.*)

BABINOT: He's got a nerve, that guy.

BOULANGER: Shut up, Babinot.

FATHER MICHEL: Come on, hurry up! Now we'll jog back to
school.

22

JULIEN *is sleeping. A quiet but persistent sound wakes him. He opens
his eyes.* BONNET *has set up two candles on his bedside table. He is
standing at the foot of his bed, his beret on his head, and murmuring.*
JULIEN, *his eyes open wide now, stares at the silhouette trembling in
the candlelight, listens to the litany that is unlike any he has ever
heard. He turns a little, makes his bed creak.* BONNET *stops for a
moment.* JULIEN *closes his eyes.* BONNET *goes on praying.*

23

MOREAU: Bend, one, two . . . Arms back . . .

(MOREAU *is conducting the morning exercises of the lower grades. A
group of militiamen in uniform—blue jackets, crossbelts, berets—
enters the yard. A line of students jogs past them.* MOREAU *takes the
lead and directs them to another end of the yard. He makes them do
kneebends, his gaze fixed on the militiamen who are now talking to*
FATHER JEAN *outside the kitchen. Raised voices are heard.*)

FATHER JEAN: You don't have any right to come in here.

A MILITIAMAN: We have orders.

FATHER JEAN: Orders from whom?

THE MILITIAMAN: From our superiors.

FATHER JEAN: You are now within the bounds of a private institution in which there are only children and men of the cloth. I'll lodge a complaint.

THE MILITIAMAN: With who?

(The students are talking while doing their exercises.)

BABINOT: Is it the Alpine infantry?

CIRON: No, that's the militia.

BOULANGER: What do they want, those traitors?

*(*BONNET*, immobile now, looks at the militiamen. They are entering the building despite* FATHER JEAN'*s protests.* MOREAU *interrupts the exercises.)*

MOREAU: We're done. You can go back in.

(Surprised, the students break rank. MOREAU *takes the opportunity to disappear into the small side yard where the toilets are.* FATHER MICHEL *quickly orders the students back into file. He takes* BONNET *by the arm and drags him along. They join* MOREAU. JULIEN *retraces his steps and sees those three disappear behind a small door. Then he goes back to the building. The other students are already inside.* JOSEPH *is setting up trash cans.)*

JOSEPH: Something happened to your preserves. You got any more?

JULIEN: What's going on? What do they want from us, those militia guys?

JOSEPH: They're nosing about. They've heard that there are some draft dodgers at this school.

JULIEN: What's that, draft dodgers?

JOSEPH: Guys who hide out because they don't want to go do their forced labor in Germany. Moreau is one of them.

JULIEN: Oh yeah?

JOSEPH: Yes sirree. And Moreau isn't his real name either. (*He taps his bad leg.*) I don't give a shit, I'm exempt.

(MME PERRIN'S *voice is heard from the kitchen.*)

MME PERRIN: Joseph! Joseph!

(*She charges out of the kitchen like a torpedo boat.*)

JOSEPH: I'm coming! (*To* JULIEN:) She's worse than Germany.

24

In class, M. TINCHAUT *is announcing the results of the French composition test.*

M. TINCHAUT: Rollin, yours is middling. Nine and a half points. Bonnet . . . Bonnet isn't here?

SAGARD: Good riddance!

M. TINCHAUT: Quentin, thirteen. This is intelligent, but a bit pretentious. For instance: "Charles Péguy perceived the cathedral as a grand and generous beacon."

(*Laughter.* FATHER MICHEL *enters with* BONNET *and sends him off to his place next to little* NAVARRE.)

NAVARRE: Where have you been?

(FATHER MICHEL *whispers something in* TINCHAUT'S *ear, then leaves.* TINCHAUT *carries on.*)

M. TINCHAUT: Ciron, twelve. Where did you discover barges in the middle of Beauce?

CIRON: On the Foussarde Canal, sir. I went there on vacation.

M. TINCHAUT: Bonnet, I've given you thirteen and a half.

Good work. Sharp and well written. Quentin, you'll
have some competition.

(JULIEN *does not take his eyes off* BONNET, *who returns his gaze
without flinching.*)

25

Lunch is over, the students are coming out of the refectory. BONNET
and NÉGUS *pass by, talking in low voices. Close to the kitchen,*
JULIEN *sees* JOSEPH *slip some cigarettes to* FRANÇOIS, *who quickly
slips them into his pocket.*

FRANÇOIS: I can't pay you right now.

JOSEPH: But Quentin, you promised.

(FRANÇOIS, *walking away, points at his brother.*)

FRANÇOIS: Ask the little shit, I'm sure he's still got some
        sugar. He's such a miser.

(JOSEPH *catches up with* JULIEN *and digs some marbles out of his
pocket.*)

JOSEPH: Aggies. Look, I'm giving you one.

(JULIEN *lets an agate sparkle in the light.*)

A VOICE: Quentin. Julien Quentin.

(*It is a supervisor who is distributing the mail at the bottom of the
stairs.* JULIEN *pockets the marble and runs to get his letter.*)

JOSEPH: Wait!

(JULIEN *runs up the stairs, tearing the envelope.*)

26

JULIEN *enters the deserted dormitory. He sits down on his cot to read his letter.*

HIS MOTHER'S VOICE: The apartment seems empty without you. Paris isn't much fun these days. There are air raids almost every night. Yesterday, a bomb fell on a building in Boulogne-Billancourt. Eight dead. How awful! Your sisters have gone back to Sainte-Marie. Sophie works Thursdays and Sundays at the Red Cross. There are so many unfortunate people! Your father is in Lille. His factory is working overtime; he is in a foul mood. It really is time for this war to be over. I'll come and get you at eight on Sunday, as we agreed. We'll have lunch at Le Grand Cerf. I'm already rejoicing at the prospect of hugging you to my heart. Your mother who loves you. P.S. Eat your preserves. I'll bring you some more. Take good care of your health.

(JULIEN *folds the letter, raises it to his face and sniffs it, then puts it in the drawer of his bedside table. He looks around, picks up* BON-NET'S *pillow, finds two candles, rolls them between his fingertips. He gets up and opens his locker, surprising a mouse with its nose in his kilogram of sugar.*)

JULIEN: Off with you, Hortense!

(*He chases the mouse off, takes a sugar cube, and cracks it between his teeth. Then he opens another locker door a little farther away, gropes around among articles of clothing, pulls out a stack of books. In one of them he finds a photograph of* BONNET *at a younger age, sitting between a man and a woman. All three are smiling, arms linked in front of battlements—the Château d'If. He opens a book, an illustrated edition of* The Man with the Tattered Ear *by Edmond About. A piece of paper has been glued to the flyleaf. He reads: "Lycée Jules Ferry. School year 1941–1942. First prize in arithmetic.*

*Jean . . ." The rest of the name has been erased. But on the facing
page, the ink of the inscription shows it in reverse. He takes the book
over to a mirror on the wall and reads: "Jean Kippelstein." He says it,
quietly. "Kippelstein, Kippelstein," trying out different pronuncia-
tions. A bell rings. He hears footsteps and puts the book back in a
hurry.* BOULANGER *and some others enter the dormitory.*)

BOULANGER: I'm hungry.

(BONNET *comes in, talking to* NAVARRE. *He does not see* JULIEN.)

NAVARRE: What exactly is a perpendicular bisector?

BONNET: It's the perpendicular to a line segment at its center.

27

M. FLORENT, *the Greek teacher, walks around the classroom with
short steps, bent almost double, constantly rubbing his hands to warm
them. He is slowly dictating a passage from* History of the Pel-
oponnesian War *in which Thucydides relates the mutilation of the
Hermae at Athens.* JULIEN *is writing to the dictation, very fast.
After each phrase, he has a moment in which to slide* The Three
Musketeers *out from under his notebook and to read a few lines,
eagerly. He has reached the final pages of the novel.* BONNET *is not
doing Greek. He is drawing a fighter plane with tricolor markings, in
great detail. The bell rings. The students hurry to the door.* BONNET
goes on drawing.

M. FLORENT (*to* BONNET): Greek is very useful, you know.
   All the scientific words have Greek roots.

(*He leaves.* BONNET *raises his head and sees* JULIEN, *who has
hunkered down next to the stove. They are alone.* JULIEN *reads the
conclusion of* The Three Musketeers, *sighs, closes the book.*)

JULIEN: Who do you like best, Athos or d'Artagnan?

BONNET (*without raising his head*): Aramis.

JULIEN: Aramis! He's a phony.

BONNET: Yes, but he's the smartest one.

(JULIEN *comes over and looks at* BONNET's *drawing.*)

JULIEN: Why aren't you taking Greek?

BONNET: I took Latin.

JULIEN: Where was that?

BONNET: At the lycée. In Marseille.

JULIEN: You're from Marseille? You don't sound like it.

BONNET: I wasn't born there.

JULIEN: Where were you born?

BONNET: If I told you, you wouldn't know where it was. Is Greek hard?

JULIEN: Not so very hard, once you get the hang of the alphabet. Are your parents in Marseille?

(BONNET *gets up, puts away his drawing.*)

BONNET: My father's a prisoner.

JULIEN: And he hasn't escaped?

(BONNET *puts on his cape and is about to leave.* JULIEN *grabs his shoulder.*)

JULIEN: And your mother? Where is she?

(BONNET *tries to extricate himself, but* JULIEN *corners him against a desk.*)

JULIEN: You don't want to tell me where your mother is?

BONNET: She is in the unoccupied zone.

JULIEN: There no longer is an unoccupied zone.

BONNET: I know. Leave me alone! I'm not asking you things, am I . . . I don't know where she is. She hasn't written to me for three months. So, there. That make you happy?

(FATHER HIPPOLYTE *has quietly entered the room.*)

FATHER HIPPOLYTE: What are you two doing here?

JULIEN: I have a cold. I've got a cough. (*Coughs.*)

FATHER HIPPOLYTE: Out you go, no fibs. Out to recess.

(*He leaves. The two boys look at each other, both equally embarrassed.*)

JULIEN: What an asshole, that Hippo. Always snooping around.

28

The boys are playing the bandanna game. They stick Boy Scout bandannas into their belts at the back and then try to snatch them away from each other. JULIEN *wends his way through the players, looking at the ground, and joins* FRANÇOIS *by the pigpen, where the latter stands smoking cigarettes with* PESSOZ *and another senior boy. The topic is philosophy.*

FRANÇOIS: Saint Thomas just doesn't hold up. His proofs for the existence of God are specious.

PESSOZ: God exists because we have the idea of God.

FRANÇOIS: Sheer sophistry . . . Now Bergson, at least he looks for the transcendental in modern science. That's a little sharper.

(*He blows a puff of cigarette smoke at* JULIEN, *making him cough and choke. The others laugh.*)

JULIEN: That's so strong!

FRANÇOIS: That's the real stuff, you little bugger. That's not corn silk.

(*The players draw closer.* NÉGUS *grabs a bandanna and waves it above his head with cries of triumph.*)

FRANÇOIS: Come on, let's go someplace else. The *babasses* will catch us here.

(*He tosses his butt and takes* JULIEN's *arm.*)

FRANÇOIS: Do me a favor.

JULIEN: What is it?

FRANÇOIS: Pass a note to that little Davenne, your piano teacher.

JULIEN: You're nuts! I'll get into trouble.

FRANÇOIS: No, you won't. She won't tell on you. You're such a coward!

JULIEN: François—what's a kike?

FRANÇOIS: A Jew.

JULIEN: I know that! But what does that really mean?

FRANÇOIS: Someone who doesn't eat pork.

JULIEN: You're putting me on.

FRANÇOIS: No, I'm not.

JULIEN: What exactly do people blame them for?

FRANÇOIS: For being smarter than we are. And also for crucifying Jesus Christ.

JULIEN: But that isn't right. The Romans did that. And is that why they have to wear the yellow star?

FRANÇOIS: No, no . . . So you'll give my letter to Davenne?

JULIEN: I certainly won't. What do you want from her, anyway?

FRANÇOIS: None of your business! Come on, do me that favor—I'll let you have *The Arabian Nights*. They'll give you a hard-on.

(*They hear shouting and see a crowd gathering by the kitchen. JOSEPH is on the ground encircled by a group of students who are mocking him and pushing him over again as soon as he gets up.*)

A STUDENT: Joseph, you smell bad.

FATHER MICHEL: Now, now! Stop that, right now!

(*JOSEPH is furious. He throws himself at a boy.*)

JOSEPH: He's insulting me!

(*MOREAU intervenes and leads him away.*)

MOREAU: Calm down now, Joseph, and go back to the kitchen.

JOSEPH: "Down, Joseph. In the corner, Joseph"—I'm not a dog!

(*A student starts barking.*)

FATHER MICHEL: D'Arsonval, that's enough.

29

JULIEN *and* BONNET *are the youngest of the eight students from their school walking along a road in the woods—the equivalent of a scout patrol. They are wearing capes and berets, green bandannas round their necks, their belts over their capes, with another bandanna stuck in the back of the belt. They are following trail signs marked on boulders, first an arrow, farther on a cross.*

A BOY: Shit, another false trail . . .

(PESSOZ, *the patrol leader, makes them retrace their steps.*)

PESSOZ: We have to get back to the crossroads, and fast. And without a noise. Where *are* the others?

(BOULANGER, JULIEN, *and* BONNET *lag behind.* BONNET *is playing with a pine cone.* JULIEN *is daydreaming.*)

JULIEN: What's the date today?

BOULANGER: January 17, 1944. Thursday.

JULIEN: Do you realize it'll never again be January 17, 1944? Never, never, never again.

PESSOZ (*from a distance.*): Hurry up, you little guys.

JULIEN: And forty years from now, half these guys will be dead and buried.

BOULANGER: Come on, let's move it.

(*The trail winds around a big boulder, and the others disappear behind it.* BOULANGER *speeds up to catch up with them.*)

JULIEN (*to* BONNET): Seems I'm the only one at this school who thinks about death. That's really incredible.

(*They hear shouts, start running. They stop behind the boulder and see their fellow Greens a little farther away, under attack by the other patrol, the Red Bandannas. The battle is almost over.* PESSOZ *is defending himself ferociously, but the Reds surround him and take his belt bandanna.*)

A RED: You're our prisoners now. Follow us. We're going to tie your hands behind your backs.

PESSOZ: You knew we were here?

A RED: We could hear you coming a kilometer away.

OTHER REDS: There's two missing . . . Over there! That's Quentin!

(Four or five Reds run toward JULIEN *and* BONNET *and try to surround them.* JULIEN *and* BONNET *take off through the trees, running as fast as they can.* BONNET *loses ground to his pursuers and lets himself be taken prisoner.* JULIEN *makes a sudden left turn and disappears from their sight. He keeps on going a long time without looking back, until, winded, he lies down behind a boulder. He gets his breath back, holding his head in his hands and hearing calls, voices, first very close, then growing faint. Silence returns. He starts walking. His leg is hurting him and slowing him down. He finds himself on another road through the woods and sees an arrow on a tree. He smiles, proceeds in the direction of the arrow. From far off, yet another couple of whistles and calls. Night begins to fall. On a boulder, he sees a circle surrounding an arrow that points down at the ground. He looks around the boulder, sees broken branches arranged in star shapes. He digs a little and extracts a little box from the ground, a tin containing vitamin crackers and a piece of paper. He reads what it says: "You've won. The game is over. Go back the way you came."* JULIEN *straightens up, triumphant, and starts shouting at the top of his voice.)*

JULIEN: I've got the treasure! We've won! The Greens have won!

(A great silence is his answer. It is night now. The dense trees of the woods form a dark wall that surrounds him. He takes the tin and starts limping back, looking for signs that will lead him to the others, but loses his way in a maze of boulders. He opens the tin and eats a cracker. From time to time, he calls for help, but without conviction. He hears something crack, stops on the spot. Below him, a shadow hides behind a boulder. Terrified, JULIEN *shrinks back. He snaps a branch. The other one gets up, takes a look, hides again.* JULIEN *descends, walking around the boulders very fast. He is running away from the place when he hears a muffled call, his name. He goes back and sees it is* BONNET, *frozen, like himself.)*

JULIEN: They didn't catch you?

BONNET: Well, they did. They tied me to a tree, but I managed to get loose.

JULIEN: Those dirty bastards!

(JULIEN *shows him the tin.*)

JULIEN: I found the treasure. All by myself.

BONNET: Are there wolves in these woods?

(*They proceed through the undergrowth, stumbling in the dark. BONNET is whimpering, or perhaps murmuring a prayer. JULIEN has big tears on his cheeks. He is humming "Maréchal, nous voilà." BONNET joins in. They hear what sounds like a cavalcade, accompanied by grunts. They see a wild boar trotting through the trees, poking the soil with his snout. JULIEN's teeth start chattering, faster and faster. BONNET pulls him back. They fall, making branches crack. The boar runs off. At last, they come to a paved road.*)

JULIEN: It's to the right. I'm sure of that.

BONNET: But no, it's to the left!

(*They take a few steps, each one in his own direction. Then they hear the noise of an automobile engine. Two headlights are coming toward them, wartime headlights, dimmed with black paint. The light is only a thin ray. JULIEN stands in the middle of the road, raises his arms. The automobile slows down, stops. He hears German voices addressing him, rifle bolts being drawn back. BONNET panics and runs into the trees, stumbles, falls with a cry. Two Germans go and get him, pointing their Mausers at him. They laugh when they see this child on the ground, staring at them in terror.*)

30

JULIEN *and* BONNET *are squeezed between two soldiers in the backseat of the German vehicle. They are sharing a blanket and shivering. The automobile pulls into town.* THE CORPORAL *sitting next to the driver turns. His French is quite good.*

THE CORPORAL: It's right next to the church, with the big wall?

(JULIEN *nods yes*.)

THE CORPORAL (*pleased with himself*): I knew it. We Bavarians, we're Catholics.

31

FATHER HIPPOLYTE *opens the school gate for* THE CORPORAL, *who pushes ahead of him the two children still wrapped in their blanket.*

THE CORPORAL (*in a bantering tone*): Good evening, Father. Have you been missing any children?

FATHER HIPPOLYTE: We've been looking for you two everywhere. Julien, do you know what time it is? You're always doing these idiotic things.

JULIEN (*explodes*): Idiotic! That's too much. (*He holds up the tin.*) I found the treasure, and then everybody had disappeared, and then . . .

(*He dissolves into tears, furious, exhausted.* FATHER JEAN *appears, followed by a few students. He takes* JULIEN *in his arms.*)

FATHER JEAN: It's over now, little one. It's over.

A STUDENT: What happened to them?

ANOTHER STUDENT: They got themselves arrested by the *boches*.

(*Someone goes*, "*Shush!*")

THE CORPORAL (*still jocular*): Can the *boches* have their blanket back?

(FATHER JEAN *takes the blanket and hands it to the German.*)

THE CORPORAL: The woods are out of bounds to civilians after 2000 hours. Haven't you heard about the blackout?

FATHER JEAN (*irritated*): Do you think we did this on purpose? Would you like to come in and have something warm to drink?

THE CORPORAL: Thank you, but we're on patrol.

(*He salutes and returns to his car.* PESSOZ *appears.*)

PESSOZ: Listen, Quentin, I really got chewed out because of you!

JULIEN (*teeth chattering*): I made you win, you son of a bitch!

FATHER JEAN: Take them to the infirmary.

32

The infirmary is in the garret. Most of the beds are empty. BONNET, *sitting on a bed, is in the midst of an animated conversation with* NÉGUS. *A little farther off,* JULIEN *is reading, propped up on one elbow. He looks up, irritated by the laughter of* NÉGUS *and* BONNET. FRANÇOIS *enters and offers* JULIEN *a slice of bread with paté.*

FRANÇOIS: Feeling better, little jerk? Look here, I brought you a present from Joseph. And a letter. Your mother's deigned to write to me.

JULIEN: *My* mother. She's yours, too.

FRANÇOIS: Yes, but you are her little darling. Papa is in Lille all the time. I bet she's getting plenty.

JULIEN: What is that supposed to mean?

FRANÇOIS: Women, my dear, they're whores, all of them. Oh
   I'm sorry, Sister . . .

(*He pirouettes around the nurse and is gone.*)

JULIEN: What an imbecile!

(*He takes his mother's letter and reads it. The nurse, a Carmelite
sister with a beauty spot on her chin from which hairs grow,
approaches* JULIEN *carrying a bottle filled with a violet liquid.*)

THE NURSE: Time to paint your throat.

JULIEN: Again!

THE NURSE: Three times a day.

(*She plunges a wooden stick tipped with a cotton swab into the bottle.
JULIEN goes on reading the letter.*)

THE NURSE: Open your mouth . . . Wider, wider.

(*With one hand she depresses his tongue with a spoon; with the other
she vigorously swabs the inside of his throat, indeed painting it all the
way to the larynx. JULIEN gags, coughs, protests. CIRON and
BOULANGER are standing at the foot of the bed.*)

BOULANGER: You must've been scared shitless last night!

JULIEN: We weren't that scared.

CIRON: We heard you saw some wild boar? Were there a lot of
   them?

(JULIEN *looks at* BONNET, *who has joined them.*)

JULIEN: Oh, about fifty.

BOULANGER: And the Germans? Did they fire at you?

JULIEN: Just a few bursts.

CIRON: You're kidding!

(*He picks up* JULIEN's *book.*)

CIRON: What are you reading?

JULIEN: It's *The Arabian Nights*. My brother passed it on to me. It's forbidden by the *babasses*.

CIRON: Why?

JULIEN: It's stories about sex. Really great. I'll lend it to you.

(*The bell rings.*)

THE NURSE: Recess is over.

BOULANGER: Time to get some religious instruction.

JULIEN: Kiss Mother Michel for me.

BOULANGER: Twice if not once. See you tomorrow!

(CIRON *and* BOULANGER *leave.* BONNET *catches a fly in his cupped hands. He then holds it with the fingers of one hand and gently plucks off one of its wings.*)

JULIEN: You're disgusting.

BONNET: It doesn't hurt it.

(JULIEN *takes a bite of his slice of bread with paté. He breaks it in two and offers half to* BONNET.)

BONNET: No, thanks. I don't like paté.

(JULIEN *tries to stuff some into his mouth.*)

JULIEN: Come on, eat.

(BONNET *pushes the bread away and gets up, furious.*)

BONNET: No, I tell you. I don't like paté.

JULIEN: Because it's made out of pork?

BONNET: Why are you always asking me these dumb questions?

JULIEN (*in a very low voice*): Because your name is Kippelstein, not Bonnet. Tell me, is it Kippelstein or Kippelsteen?

(BONNET *lunges at him.* THE NURSE *sees it and separates them.*)

THE NURSE: Bonnet, if you don't get into bed this very instant, I'm going to send you back down.

(BONNET *returns to his bed.* JULIEN, *without taking his eyes off him, finishes his slice of bread.*)

33

At their washbasins, the students are in their Sunday best, coats and ties. JULIEN *checks himself in the mirror, very carefully. He wets his hair, parts it, all with a touch of narcissism.*

JULIEN (*to the boy next to him*): Your parents coming?

THE OTHER BOY (*with a sigh*): *Everybody* is coming . . .

(BONNET *comes from his ablutions, wearing everyday clothes.*)

JULIEN (*happily*): Aren't you getting dressed up? Don't you have any visitors?

BONNET: What's it to you?

34

The pews in the chapel are full. All the teachers are there, and many parents, sitting next to their offspring. MME QUENTIN *is sitting with* FRANÇOIS *and* JULIEN. BONNET, NÉGUS, *and* DUPRÉ *are by themselves, in the back, a little like pariahs. Applause. Every-*

body sits back down. FATHER JEAN, *who is officiating, steps forward to address the congregation.*

FATHER JEAN: Today, I'm addressing myself especially to the youngest among you who will take their first communion in a few weeks from now. My children, we are living in times of discord and hatred. The lie is all-powerful; Christians are killing other Christians; those who should lead us, betray us. More than ever, we have to be on guard against egoism and indifference. You all come from privileged, in some cases very privileged, families. Because much has been given to you, much will be asked of you. Remember the stern words of the Gospel: "It is easier for a camel to go through the eye of a needle than for a rich man to enter the kingdom of God." And Saint James: "Come now, you rich! Weep and howl for the miseries that are coming upon you. Your riches have rotted and your garments are moth-eaten . . ." Material riches corrupt souls and desiccate hearts. They turn people suspicious, unjust, and pitiless in their egoism. How well I understand the anger of those who have nothing, while the rich feast so arrogantly.

(This diatribe evokes some reaction.)

MME QUENTIN: Strong words!

(A well-dressed gentleman gets up and leaves the chapel. Impassively, FATHER JEAN *waits until the man has left.)*

FATHER JEAN: I have not wanted to shock you but only remind you that charity is the first duty of a Christian. In today's Epistle, Saint Paul tells us: "Brethren, do not think you are all-knowing. Do not return harm for harm. If your enemy is hungry, give him food. If he is thirsty, give him drink." We shall pray for those who are suffering, those who are hungry, those who are being persecuted. We shall pray for the victims, and for their tormentors as well.

(*Later. Communion. Students and parents go to receive the conse-crated Host.* JULIEN *walks up, hands crossed, eyes down.* BONNET *leaves his seat and joins the line despite* NÉGUS, *who tries to hold him back. He kneels next to* JULIEN. FATHER JEAN *approaches them, the ciborium in his hand. He holds out the wafer toward* BONNET'S *lips. When he recognizes* BONNET, *his hand stops. There is a rapid exchange of glances between* BONNET, JULIEN, *and* FATHER JEAN. *He places the host on* JULIEN'S *tongue and moves on.*)

35

After Mass, parents and students stand in the schoolyard in small groups, conversing with the fathers and the teachers. MME QUENTIN *is talking with* FATHER JEAN. FRANÇOIS *is standing next to* MLLE DAVENNE *in her Sunday finery.* JULIEN *and some other boys are engaging in simulated bouts of French boxing, hitting each other with their feet, legs raised high. They are excited, their voices loud as they are unruly in front of their parents.* CIRON *and* BABINOT *are circling* BONNET, *who is watching them.*

BABINOT: *En garde*, Dubonnet, *en garde*.

(BONNET *receives a kick in the buttock. Furious, he attacks* BABINOT. CIRON *grabs him from behind.*)

CIRON: Help me, you guys. Let's give it to the Huguenot.

(*In the melee that ensues,* BONNET *cuffs* JULIEN, *who grabs hold of him and trips him.* BONNET *falls to the ground with him, and they roll on the ground, furiously pummeling each other.* MME QUENTIN *rushes to the scene.*)

MME QUENTIN: Julien, have you lost your mind! Your beau-tiful suit . . .

(*The boys get up.* JULIEN *brushes off his coat. One of its sleeves is torn.*)

MME QUENTIN: What will they think at the restaurant!

(BONNET *looks at* JULIEN *and laughs.* JULIEN, *too, starts laughing.*)

MME QUENTIN: What's the matter with you? You think that's funny?

(*The scene degenerates into crazy, contagious laughter, and* MME QUENTIN *is finally unable to resist and joins in.* JULIEN *whispers something in his mother's ear.*)

36

Le Grand Cerf is the town's one elegant restaurant. Several tables are taken up by Wehrmacht officers. MME QUENTIN *is ordering. Seated with her are* FRANÇOIS, JULIEN, *and* BONNET, *who is watching* THE QUENTINS *as if he were in a theater.*

MME QUENTIN: What do you have in the way of fish?

THE MAÎTRE D': We haven't had any fish for a long time, madam. I recommend the *lapin chasseur*. It's half a meat-ration coupon per portion.

FRANÇOIS: Is it really rabbit, or is it cat?

THE MAÎTRE D': It is rabbit, sir. With browned potatoes.

MME QUENTIN: Are they buttered, your potatoes?

THE MAÎTRE D': We use margarine, madam. No coupons required.

(MME QUENTIN *looks at her sons, makes a funny face.*)

MME QUENTIN: The *lapin chasseur* it is, then. And a bottle of Bordeaux.

(THE MAÎTRE D' *leaves.* MME QUENTIN *looks around. The Germans at the next table are talking loudly and eyeing her. One of them raises his glass to her.*)

MME QUENTIN (*whispers*): A lot of uniforms here today. I thought they were all at the Russian front.

FRANÇOIS: You've caught their eye.

MME QUENTIN (*to* BONNET): Your parents weren't able to come?

BONNET: No, madam.

MME QUENTIN: Poor little fellow.

FRANÇOIS: What about Papa? He said he would be here.

MME QUENTIN: Something came up. Problems at the factory.

JULIEN: What else is new . . .

MME QUENTIN: Your father has some crushing responsibilities to bear, at this time.

FRANÇOIS: Is he still in favor of Pétain?

MME QUENTIN: Nobody is in favor of Pétain anymore! (*To* JULIEN:) They told me what happened to you in the woods. And I really gave Father Jean a piece of my mind! These Boy Scout games are ridiculous, now that it's so cold. God knows what could have happened to you, my poor little darling. Bullets can start flying so easily!

(*She strokes his cheek.* JULIEN *shrinks back.*)

FRANÇOIS: It builds his character.

MME QUENTIN: That's exactly what Father Jean told me. Builds his character! What do you think of *that*?

JULIEN (*pointing at* BONNET): He was in the woods with me.

(MME QUENTIN *smiles at* BONNET.)

MME QUENTIN: I assume you're from Lyon. All the Gillets are from Lyon, and they manufacture all the silk.

JULIEN: His name is Bonnet, not Gillet. And he's from Marseille.

MME QUENTIN (*taps her head*): But of course! I knew a Marie-Claire Bonnet from Marseille, she was a cousin of the Du Perrons, the oil people. Is she your mother?

BONNET: No, madam. My family is not in oil.

MME QUENTIN: But that's strange.

JULIEN: Bonnet's father is a bookkeeper.

MME QUENTIN: I see!

(*Alone at his table, a very elegant old gentleman asks for his check.* THE MAÎTRE D' *treats him like an old patron.*)

THE MAÎTRE D': Right away, Monsieur Meyer. Did you enjoy your lunch?

MEYER (*smiles*): Thank you, yes. The *lapin* was acceptable.

(*Two militiamen in uniform have entered the restaurant and are checking tables. The younger one approaches* MEYER.)

THE MILITIAMAN: Your papers, sir.

(M. MEYER *puts out his cigarette, takes out his wallet, shows his identity card.* THE MILITIAMAN *glances at it.*)

THE MILITIAMAN (*very loud*): Hey, listen, can't you read? This restaurant is out of bounds to yids.

(*A great hush falls over the restaurant.* JULIEN *looks at* BONNET, *who is looking at* MEYER.)

MME QUENTIN: Why do they have to bother people like that? That gentleman looks so presentable.

(THE MAÎTRE D' *approaches*.)

THE MAÎTRE D': M. Meyer has been coming here for twenty years. I cannot refuse service to him.

THE MILITIAMAN: Shut up, flunky. I can have your license revoked.

FRANÇOIS (*under his breath*): Collaborators!

(*The other militiaman moves toward him. He is old and fat and sports a moustache.*)

THE MILITIAMAN: Was it you who said that?

MME QUENTIN: Be quiet, François! (*To* THE MILITIAMAN:) He's a child. He doesn't know what he's saying.

THE MILITIAMAN: Madam, we serve France, our country. This lad has insulted us.

(*There is some commotion in the room, as if those present were picking up their courage.*)

A WOMAN: Leave the old man alone. You're doing a shameful thing.

(*Other voices are raised: "Come on . . . You don't have the right . . ."*)

A VOICE (*strident*): They're right. Send the Jews to Moscow!

(*A German voice rises above the brouhaha: "Get the hell out!" Silence. Behind* THE QUENTINS, *an officer has risen to his feet. He is wearing one arm in a sling, a monocle, and many decorations. He is drunk and is having difficulty standing upright. He walks over to* THE OLDER MILITIAMAN *and glares at him. He is a head taller than* THE MILITIAMAN.)

THE OFFICER: You heard me? Get the hell out.

(THE MILITIAMAN *looks at him, hesitates. Finally, he salutes the German and retires with his young colleague in tow.*)

THE YOUNG MILITIAMAN (*to* MEYER): We'll meet again.

(*The German slumps back into his chair. Conversations are resumed.*)

MME QUENTIN: They can say what they want, but some of them are good people.

FRANÇOIS: He did that to impress you.

(BONNET *watches* MEYER *put his wallet back into his coat pocket.*)

JULIEN (*brusquely*): We're not Jews?

MME QUENTIN: That would take the cake!

JULIEN: What about Aunt Reinach? Isn't that a Jewish name?

MME QUENTIN: The Reinachs are from Alsace.

FRANÇOIS: Well, they could be from Alsace *and* Jewish.

MME QUENTIN: That's enough, thank you. The Reinachs are *very* Catholic. If they could hear you! Mind you, I have nothing against Jews. On the contrary. Except for that Léon Blum, of course. He deserves hanging. Julien, sit up straight.

37

A Sunday atmosphere in the streets of the little town. A lemonade vendor can be heard. MME QUENTIN *and* JULIEN *are walking side by side, her arm around his shoulders.*

MME QUENTIN: He is nice, your friend, but he doesn't say much.

JULIEN (*pompously*): He has his reasons.

MME QUENTIN: Then he's not dumb?

JULIEN: Not in the least.

(MME QUENTIN *laughs and turns to look back.*)

MME QUENTIN: What happened to François?

(*A short distance behind them,* FRANÇOIS *is giving directions to a group of German soldiers.*)

FRANÇOIS: You just go past the church and then keep going, straight ahead, until you get to the bridge . . .

(*The Germans thank him effusively.*)

JULIEN: He's sending them in the opposite direction. He always does that to the uniforms.

MME QUENTIN: Very clever!

(FRANÇOIS *rejoins them. He is slightly inebriated.*)

FRANÇOIS: What would you say if I joined the underground?

MME QUENTIN: Don't say such things. You have to graduate.

FRANÇOIS: Graduate, graduate. There're more important things . . . Has Julien told you he wants to become a *babasse*?

JULIEN: I don't want to become a *babasse*. I want to become a missionary in the Congo.

MME QUENTIN: I forbid you to use that stupid word *babasse*. It's disgraceful. You should be full of gratitude toward these poor monks who are undermining their health trying to give you an education.

(FRANÇOIS *and* JULIEN *finish the sentence in unison with their mother.*)

MME QUENTIN: I mean it!

(FRANÇOIS *grabs* JULIEN'S *elbow:* JOSEPH, *in his Sunday best, comes out of an alley, arm-in-arm with a heavily made-up girl.*)

THE GIRL: You really get on my nerves! Boy, do you ever! Leave me alone!

(*She lets go of his arm and turns around.* JOSEPH *runs after her.*)

JOSEPH: Fernande, Fernande!

FRANÇOIS *and* JULIEN: Fernande! Fernande!

MME QUENTIN: You know her?

(*The brothers giggle.*)

MME QUENTIN: My dear Julien, are you really sure you want to become a priest?

JULIEN: Is that against your convictions?

MME QUENTIN: Absolutely not. Your father and I would be very proud of you. But I would so like for you to go to the Polytechnique like your grandfather.

FRANÇOIS: Don't you worry. He'll fall in love and get defrocked. He's a real sentimental guy, just like Joseph.

(JULIEN *punches him. The brothers exchange blows. They pass another family from the school: the son, the parents, and the sister, a pretty young girl of seventeen. The girl's and* FRANÇOIS' *eyes meet. The latter whispers to his brother.*)

FRANÇOIS: She really is a dish, Laviron's sister. I'm going to sweet-talk her.

(*He turns around and joins* THE LAVIRONS. MME QUENTIN *consults her watch. She goes to* JULIEN *and hugs him to her.* JULIEN *disengages himself.*)

MME QUENTIN: I see, no more cuddling . . . What do you know, you've got a bit of a moustache.

JULIEN: What if I went back to Paris with you? Papa wouldn't
have to know.

(*She looks at him, disconcerted. She folds him in her arms.*)

38

BONNET *and some other students are going down the stairs of the*
school. They pass JULIEN, *who is carrying three jars of preserves and*
looking glum. BONNET *turns and catches up with him.*

BONNET: She's nice, your mother. Boy, does she talk fast!

JULIEN: She's crazy.

BONNET: You'll see her again soon. You'll be leaving for
Mardi Gras.

39

The end of dinner. Students and teachers are moving the refectory
tables and putting up a screen for the weekly movie session. FATHER
MICHEL *is setting up the projector under the critical eye of*
MOREAU.

MOREAU: If you do that, you'll have the film break the way it
did the other time.

FATHER MICHEL: I'm very familiar with this machine!

(*Still at a table,* BONNET *and* JULIEN *are sharing a jar of preserves,*
which they are heaping onto crackers.)

BONNET: Great preserves!

JULIEN: Adrienne made them.

BONNET: Adrienne is your sister?

JULIEN: No, she's the cook . . . What's so funny? Don't you have a cook?

BONNET: No, we don't.

JULIEN: You eat out all the time?

BONNET (*laughing*): Oh no! My mother cooks very well.

(*Two big boys come up to take the bench on which they are seated.*)

A BIG BOY: Come on, shrimps, move it.

JOSEPH: Hey, those are my preserves you're wolfing.

JULIEN: Sure, sure.

(M. FLORENT *is tuning his violin. He is going to accompany Charlie Chaplin's silent images with the assistance of* MLLE DAVENNE *at the piano.* BONNET *and* JULIEN *are sitting next to each other. The lights go out, the projector starts clicking, and the title of the movie,* The Immigrant, *appears on the screen.* M. FLORENT *and* MLLE DAVENNE *get going on the* Rondo Capriccioso *by Saint-Saëns. The pathos of the music corresponds with Chaplin's gentle comedy. The children are enthralled; it is a tender moment, a moment of forgetfulness.* FRANÇOIS *is standing next to* MLLE DAVENNE *and turning the pages of the sheet music. When a chase scene occurs,* M. FLORENT *embarks on a rapid movement. The audience laughs a lot. They know the movie by heart and announce its gags in advance. The two laughing hardest are* JOSEPH *and* FATHER JEAN, *side by side. It is surprising to see this austere man of the cloth bent over double, bursting into laughter, slapping his thighs at the antics of the little clown. The music grows calmer, and Chaplin becomes sentimental again. He is courting lovely Edna Purviance. Both children and teachers become dreamy-eyed. A sharp little cry, a scuffle in the near dark.* FRANÇOIS *is trying to kiss* MLLE DAVENNE, *but she won't let him. The immigrant ship enters New*

York harbor. NÉGUS, BONNET, *and* JULIEN *see the Statue of Liberty appear on the screen.*)

40

Dawn is just beginning to break through the dormitory windows. The boys are fast asleep on their cots. No one moves. A muffled exclamation—"Shit"—is heard. JULIEN *stretches, slips his hand under the covers.*

JULIEN: And shit again . . .

(*He opens up the covers and rubs the damp stain with his towel. This time, he is observed from behind by* SAGARD. MOREAU *enters and switches on the light.*)

MOREAU: Time to get up.

(JULIEN *covers up the sheet in haste and pretends to be busy getting dressed, but* SAGARD *retrieves the towel with the tips of his fingers and waves it about.*)

SAGARD: Quentin pees in bed. Quentin pees in bed.

(JULIEN *throws himself at* SAGARD *and knocks him to the floor, retrieving his towel. But the other boys form a circle around* JULIEN *and start chanting.*)

THE BOYS: Quentin pees in bed. Quentin pees in bed.

(JULIEN, *humiliated, mad with rage, attacks them.* BONNET *is by his side, the two of them against all the others.*)

41

At the washbasins, JULIEN *confides in* BONNET, *all the while brushing his teeth.*

JULIEN: It's the same every time. I'm in the middle of some amazing dream, I feel like I have to take a leak, I open my fly, everything is just fine. And then I wake up, and the hot piss is running all over me. Let me tell you, it isn't funny.

42

Recess. Snow is falling in the schoolyard. JULIEN *is teaching* BON-NET *how to walk on stilts.* BONNET *wobbles and falls.*

JULIEN: All right, get back up. Don't be scared.

SAGARD (*in passing*): Bedwetter.

(JULIEN *chases him.*)

JULIEN: Listen, Sagard, you asshole, I'm going to beat the shit out of you!

(*Roars are heard. Voluminous* MME PERRIN *surges out of the kitchen in pursuit of* JOSEPH, *whom she is slapping with a dishrag.*)

MME PERRIN: You rat, you dirty rat! I'll show you . . .

(*It looks like the movie of the night before, and the students laugh, but the cook is truly furious. Having had a glass or two under her belt, she stumbles but manages not to fall. She sees* FATHER MICHEL *among the stilt walkers.*)

MME PERRIN: Father Michel, Father Michel! I caught him stealing lard. He was sticking it into his bag so he could go and sell it. I told you he's a thief . . . Thief, thief, dirty rat!

(*While she is talking she goes on slapping* JOSEPH, *whom she has backed up against a wall. He raises his arms to protect himself. He seems terrified.*)

JOSEPH: That's not true, she's lying! She's the one who steals!

(*The games have stopped; everybody is watching.* FATHER MICHEL *takes* JOSEPH *by the arm and leads him toward the kitchen.*)

FATHER MICHEL: Not in front of the children, Madame Perrin. Go back to your kitchen and calm down.

FRANÇOIS (*to* JULIEN): I told that cretin he was going to get caught.

(*They look up and see* FATHER JEAN, *who is observing the scene from his office window.*)

43

Seven students from different grades are lined up in FATHER JEAN'S *office,* FRANÇOIS *and* JULIEN *among them.*

FATHER JEAN: Joseph was stealing school provisions and reselling them on the black market. Mme Perrin should have told us about this sooner, and I don't think she is innocent. But that's not all.

(*He points at the tins of paté, the candy, and the preserve jars on his desk.*)

FATHER JEAN: We found all these in his locker. These are personal provisions. And he named the seven of you.

(*He picks up a tin of paté.*)

FATHER JEAN: Which one of you had this paté?

A STUDENT: It's mine.

FATHER JEAN: And these preserves?

JULIEN: Mine.

FATHER JEAN: You know what you are? You're a thief, just like Joseph.

JULIEN: I didn't steal them. They were mine, those preserves.

FATHER JEAN: You deprived your schoolmates of them. (*To everybody:*) As far as I can see, education, true education consists of teaching you to make good use of your freedom. And this is the result! You disgust me. There's nothing I despise more than the black market. Money, always money.

FRANÇOIS: We weren't making money. We were just trading.

(FATHER JEAN *steps up to him, a hard expression on his face.*)

FATHER JEAN: Trading for what?

FRANÇOIS (*after a moment's hesitation*): Cigarettes.

FATHER JEAN: Quentin, if I didn't know all the problems this would cause your parents, I'd show you the door this minute, you and your brother. I have to fire Joseph, but this is an injustice. There will be no vacation for any of you until Easter. You can return to your studies.

(*The students leave.* FRANÇOIS *whispers to* JULIEN.)

FRANÇOIS: We got off lightly.

(*In the corridor they run into* JOSEPH, *who is waiting with* FATHER MICHEL, *leaning against the wall. He is sobbing like a kid.*)

JOSEPH: And where will I go? I don't even have a place to
    sleep.

(*The students are deeply embarrassed.* JULIEN *puts his hand on*
JOSEPH's *shoulder.*)

FATHER MICHEL: Go to class.

(*The students move on. At the end of the corridor,* JULIEN *turns and
sees* FATHER JEAN, *who appears in the doorway of his office.*)

FATHER JEAN (*to* JOSEPH): Go see the bursar. He'll pay you
    for the month.

JOSEPH: So it's just me taking the rap. It's not fair.

FATHER MICHEL: Come on, Joseph, let's go.

(*He leads him away under the eyes of* FATHER JEAN, *who seems to be
regretting the decision he has made.*)

44

BONNET *opens the door to the chapel, which is deserted. He takes a
few steps, stops, pulls his beret over his head. Defiance? Prayer? We do
not know.* JULIEN *and the other seventh-graders enter, one after the
other, making a lot of noise.* FATHER MICHEL *appears behind them,
his arms full of flowers.*

FATHER MICHEL: What's going on here?

BOULANGER: Choral practice with Mlle Davenne.

FATHER MICHEL: Well, that's handy. You and Babinot are
    going to help me arrange these flowers for Sunday.

(JULIEN *is the only one who notices* BONNET, *who is hiding behind
a pillar, still wearing his beret. Their eyes meet.* MLLE DAVENNE
comes running in. She sits down at the harmonium.)

MLLE DAVENNE: All right! Let's try it again. "I believe in Thee, my Lord . . ."

(*She looks around.*)

MLLE DAVENNE: Bonnet isn't here?

(JULIEN *turns around quickly.*)

JULIEN: No, mademoiselle. He's at the infirmary.

MLLE DAVENNE: Oh well.

(*They start singing: "I believe in Thee, my Lord, I believe in Thee . . ."*)

45

BONNET *is playing boogie-woogie on the piano in the music room. He stops and shows* JULIEN *how to embellish the low notes.*

BONNET: See, it's easy. With your left hand you go like this.

(JULIEN *tries. He is interrupted by the deafening sound of air raid sirens.*)

BONNET: We have to go to the shelter.

(*Whistles are blown, there are calls, running footsteps approaching.* JULIEN *pulls* BONNET *behind the piano.* MOREAU *comes in for a second, thinks the room is empty, and disappears again.*)

JULIEN: They won't know we're missing. They never take a count.

(*Later. Standing up at the keyboard, they are playing a four-handed boogie.* JULIEN *is doing the bass,* BONNET *is improvising on the high notes. Peals of laughter.*)

46

The school seems abandoned. There are only the two boys' silhouettes in the middle of the snow-covered yard. JULIEN *and* BONNET *are listening to the heavy sounds of bombers and the dry hacking of German antiaircraft guns.*

BONNET: I hope the Americans land soon.

JULIEN: Are you going to stay in this school even after the war is over?

BONNET: I don't know . . . I don't think so.

(*A tremor seems to run through his entire body.*)

JULIEN: Are you afraid?

BONNET: All the time.

47

In the kitchen, BONNET *and* JULIEN *are taking advantage of the air raid by roasting chestnuts. Peeling them, they burn their fingers.*

JULIEN: How long is it since you last saw him?

BONNET: My father? It's almost two years now.

JULIEN: I never get to see my father, either.

(*He grabs* BONNET'*s arm and both of them dash under the big kitchen table.* JOSEPH *comes into the kitchen. He opens a drawer and rummages around in it, his back turned to the boys.* JULIEN *gets up.*)

JULIEN: Joseph, what are you doing here?

(JOSEPH *gives a start.*)

JOSEPH: I forgot some things. What about you, what are you
   doing here?

(*He limps off. The two friends exchange smiles.*)

48

*All the students are sleeping. At the end of the dorm, a flashlight
pierces the dark.* BONNET *is stretched out listening to* JULIEN, *who
is sitting at the foot of the bed reading a passage from* The Arabian
Nights.

JULIEN: "And with a quick motion she threw off her veils and
   disrobed completely to show herself in her native naked-
   ness. Blessed be the womb that bore her! The beauty of
   the Princess was sweet and white as a linen cloth, from
   every pore she exuded the pleasing perfume of amber-
   gris, just as the rose secretes its original scent. Nour took
   her in his arms and found in her, having explored her
   intimate depths, a pearl still untouched. And he let his
   hand wander over her charming limbs and her delicate
   neck, plunged it into her opulent hair. She, in turn, was
   not slow in demonstrating the gifts she possessed. Truly,
   she combined the lascivious movements of Arab girls
   with the heat of the Ethiopians, the startled candor of the
   Franks with the consummate science of the Indians, the
   coquetry of the women of Yemen with the muscular
   vigor of the women of Upper Egypt, the delicacy of
   organs of the Chinese with the ardor of the daughters of
   Hedjza. Embraces yielded to kisses, kisses to caresses,
   and copulations to swivings until, fatigued by their
   transports and their manifold frolics, they finally fell

asleep in each other's arms, drunk with pleasure. Thus ends . . ."

(JULIEN *raises his head.* BONNET *has fallen asleep.*)

49

In the classroom, M. GUIBOURG *relates the news of the war, using a pointer on the map of Europe, on which little flags mark the respective positions of the armies.*

M. GUIBOURG: The Russians have launched a big offensive in the Ukraine. According to Radio London, the Red Army has broken through the German front 100 kilometers west of Kiev. According to Radio Paris, this offensive has been repulsed with heavy casualties. The truth probably lies somewhere in between.

(BONNET *raises his head. Through the window he can see* MOREAU *come running and then entering the building on the opposite side.*)

JULIEN *and* BOULANGER (*quietly*): Radio Paris tells, Radio Paris tells lies, Radio Paris tells German lies.

M. GUIBOURG: In Italy, on the other hand, the Americans and the British are not making any headway at Monte Cassino. Take out your notebooks. We'll do an algebra exercise.

(*He writes a formula on the blackboard. A student farts. Laughter.* M. GUIBOURG *does not turn around.*)

SAGARD: Permission to go, sir? It's this school soup.

M. GUIBOURG: Always you, Sagard, isn't it. Go ahead.

(SAGARD *leaves. A German voice is heard:* "Halt!" SAGARD *reenters the classroom backwards, pushed by a big German military policeman wearing a helmet. He also wears an olive-green raincoat and a metal breastplate and carries a submachine gun slung across his back. He sends* SAGARD *back to his place.* JULIEN *and all the others stare at the soldier, who steps aside to make way for a small man wearing a maroon coat. This man walks past the desks and stops in front of the teacher, giving him a curt salute.*)

THE MAN: Doktor Muller, of the Gestapo at Melun.

(*He turns to face the students.*)

MULLER: Which one of you is Jean Kippelstein?

(*He speaks good French, with a strong accent. The students exchange looks.* JULIEN, *his face impassive, lowers his eyes.*)

MULLER: Answer me!

M. GUIBOURG: There is no one by that name in this class.

(MULLER *starts pacing between the students' desks, scrutinizing the boys' faces. He turns, sees the map of Europe with its little flags. He walks over and rips out the Russian and American flags. Now he has his back to* JULIEN, *who can't help looking in the direction of* BONNET *for a fraction of a second.* MULLER *turns, intercepts that look. He walks slowly across the classroom and stops in front of* BONNET. BONNET *looks at him for a long moment. Then, without a word, he gets up. He is white in the face, but very calm. He arranges his books and notebooks in a very neat pile on top of his desk, goes to get his coat and beret from their hook on the wall. He shakes hands with the students next to him, still not saying a word.* MULLER *shouts an order in German. The military policeman takes* BONNET'S *arm, preventing him from shaking hands with* JULIEN, *and gives him a brutal shove to move on. They leave the room. After a few seconds, the silence is broken by* MULLER.)

MULLER: This boy is not a Frenchman. This boy is a Jew. Your teachers have committed a serious crime by hiding

him. The school is closed. You have two hours to pack
and then line up in the yard.

(*He leaves in haste. The class remains stunned for a moment.* FATHER
MICHEL *enters, talks to* M. GUIBOURG *in a low voice. Then the
room explodes with questions. Everybody gets up except for* JULIEN,
who sits staring straight ahead.)

THE STUDENTS: What is going on? Where are they taking
Bonnet?

FATHER MICHEL: Calm down and listen to me. They have
arrested Father Jean. It seems we have been denounced.

(*A loud murmur erupts from the boys.*)

JULIEN: And Bonnet?

FATHER MICHEL: Bonnet, Dupré, and Lafarge are Israelites.
Father Jean took them in at this school because their lives
were in danger. Now you will go to the dormitory and
pack your suitcases, fast and with no fuss. I'm counting
on you. First, we'll say a prayer for Father Jean and for
your classmates.

(*He has them recite the Lord's Prayer.*)

50

The students are getting packed, very fast and without a word.
JULIEN *fills his knapsack and sits down on his bed. Someone comes in
and whispers something. In low voices, the rumor travels up to*
JULIEN.

BABINOT: Négus got away.

(FRANÇOIS *walks into the dormitory carrying his knapsack, looking
for* JULIEN.)

JULIEN: They didn't get Négus.

FRANÇOIS: I know. They're looking for him, him and Moreau. They found some Resistance pamphlets in Father Jean's office.

(FATHER HIPPOLYTE *claps his hands.*)

FATHER HIPPOLYTE: Those of you who are ready, take your things and go to the refectory. Quentin, pack Laviron's knapsack and take it to him at the infirmary. Hurry.

FRANÇOIS: You want me to help you?

(JULIEN *shakes his head and starts emptying* LAVIRON's *locker. The others leave.* JULIEN *is alone in the dormitory when* BONNET *comes in with a military policeman.*)

THE GERMAN: *Schnell!*

(BONNET *goes to his locker and gathers up his clothes, avoiding* JULIEN's *eyes, his friend having moved closer to him.* THE GERMAN *lights a cigarette, turning his back to them for a moment.*)

BONNET: Don't sweat it. They would have caught up with me in any case.

JULIEN: They haven't caught up with Négus.

BONNET: I know.

(*He hands* JULIEN *a stack of books.*)

BONNET: Take these. I've read them all.

(JULIEN *pulls a book from under his mattress.*)

JULIEN: Would you like to have *The Arabian Nights*?

(BONNET *takes the book and crams it into his suitcase.* THE GERMAN *turns around.*)

THE GERMAN: *Schnell, Jude!*

(BONNET *closes his suitcase and hurries up to him.*)

51

JULIEN *comes into the infirmary, carrying* LAVIRON'*s knapsack. The infirmary nurse is very agitated.*

THE NURSE: What are you doing here? Get out!

JULIEN: I brought his sack.

(*He sets it down next to* LAVIRON. *The other beds are empty.*)

JULIEN: Are you going to get up?

(*Instead of replying,* LAVIRON *sits up and nods his head in the direction of a small door. The infirmary is in the garret, and it is connected to the granary loft. Behind the door,* MOREAU'*s head appears. He signals to the nurse, who makes a gesture of irritation.*)

THE NURSE: What else do you want?

MOREAU: We can't stay here. They'll search the attic.

(*He runs to the front door, opens it. German voices can be heard approaching on the stairs. He turns back, fetches* NÉGUS *from the granary, and makes him get into one of the beds, fully dressed.*)

MOREAU: Sister, give me a compress, fast!

THE NURSE: Leave me alone. You'll get us all arrested.

(MOREAU *has just enough time to slip into a closet. The door opens, a military policeman enters, walks into the room.* NÉGUS *pulls the covers up to his nose.* THE NURSE *drops the compress she has been holding in her hand. She is literally shaking and has to sit down.* THE GERMAN *looks at her, picks up the compress, and hands it to her. Another soldier appears through the granary door. They talk while looking around.*)

THE FIRST GERMAN (*sniffing*): There is a Jew here, I just know it.

(JULIEN *takes a step forward.*)

JULIEN: We haven't seen anybody.

(*The Germans turn and look at him. He's in a tight spot.*)

THE SECOND GERMAN: You, come here. Let your pants down.

(JULIEN *unbuckles his belt. He sees the other German, who has been leaning over the nurse, straighten up and walk over to* NÉGUS. *Abruptly, he tears off the covers, exposing the fully clothed boy.* THE GERMAN *bursts out laughing, grabs* NÉGUS *by the ear, and yanks him out of bed. Now his colleague is by his side, holding a pistol in his hand. They leave, the soldier still holding* NÉGUS *by the ear.* MOREAU *steps out of the closet.*)

MOREAU: What happened?

JULIEN: It's her.

THE NURSE (*almost in hysterics*): Go to hell!

MOREAU: I'll go across the roof and jump down into the convent garden. Goodbye, Julien.

(*He hugs the boy, goes into the granary, opens a fanlight, and slides out onto the roof.*)

52

JULIEN *charges down the stairs, opens a door, and stops in the middle of a small yard, looking up. He sees* MOREAU'S *silhouette move to the other side of the roof and disappear.* JULIEN *smiles. Hearing a voice, he turns around quickly. Two people have been hiding in a corner of the little yard. One of them comes over to* JULIEN *and addresses him in German. The other remains in the shadows; we can barely make out his face.*

JULIEN: Joseph!

(JOSEPH *detaches himself from the wall and comes over to* JULIEN.)

JOSEPH (*to* THE GERMAN): He's a friend.

THE GERMAN: *Zwei Minuten.*

JULIEN: What are you doing with *them?*

(JOSEPH *offers his cigarette to* JULIEN, *who hesitates, then takes it.* JOSEPH *lights another one.*)

JOSEPH: It's all right with you, isn't it? You'll get a vacation.

(JULIEN *stares at him, hard, as if refusing to admit the evidence of his senses.*)

JOSEPH: It's not such a big deal. Those are just Jews . . .

(JULIEN *is holding the cigarette between his fingers without smoking it.*)

JOSEPH: You really liked that Bonnet?

(JULIEN *shrinks back, still staring at* JOSEPH, *who abruptly grabs him by the shoulder.*)

JOSEPH: Don't act so pious! It's all your fault. If I hadn't done business with you guys, I wouldn't have been fired. La Perrin was stealing more stuff than I was.

(JULIEN *frees himself and runs toward the door.*)

JOSEPH (*from afar*): No need to act so pious, I'm telling you. That's war for you, old boy.

(JULIEN *turns for a moment, then flees.*)

53

MULLER *and some German military policemen come out of the building and walk out into the courtyard where all the students are lining up. It is freezing cold; the boys are jumping in place in order to keep warm.*

MULLER: Are there any more Jews among you?

(*Deep silence is his answer. Slowly,* MULLER *walks past the lined-up boys, studying their faces. He stops in front of a young boy who has black curly hair and a large mouth.*)

MULLER: So you're not a Jew? What's your name?

THE BOY: Pierre de la Rozière.

MULLER: Go stand by the wall.

(*Trembling, the boy obeys.* MULLER *gives an order in German. A military policeman steps forward, holding a stack of food-ration cards. He puts on glasses to read the names on the cards. Each student named has to go and stand by the wall.*)

THE MILITARY POLICEMAN: Abadie, Jean-Michel . . . D'Aiguillon, Emmanuel . . . Amigues, Dominique . . . Anglade, Bernard . . .

(BOULANGER, *white in the face, leans toward* JULIEN.)

BOULANGER: Do you think they'll take us too? We haven't done anything.

(*Cries, sounds of weeping interrupt the roll call. A German enters the courtyard, herding along three small girls.* MULLER *goes over to the soldier, talks to him for a moment.*)

A SMALL GIRL (*in tears*): We came to confession.

(MULLER *smiles, lets them go, and comes back to the students.*)

MULLER: That soldier was doing his duty. He had orders not

to let anyone leave. Discipline is the strength of the German soldier. What you French are lacking is discipline.

(*Then he addresses himself to the teachers lined up in front of the kitchen.*)

MULLER: We're not your enemies. You have to help us rid France of strangers, of Jews.

(*The roll call continues.*)

THE MILITARY POLICEMAN: Babinot, Jean-François . . . Bernay-Lambert, Alain . . . De Bigorre, Geoffroy . . .

(*At this moment, FATHER JEAN appears in the courtyard, wearing a cape over his robe, head bare, carrying a light suitcase. He is followed by soldiers guarding BONNET, NÉGUS, and DUPRÉ, who are also carrying bags. When the group reaches the gate to the street, FATHER JEAN turns.*)

FATHER JEAN (*in a very strong, very clear voice*): Goodbye, children! I'll be seeing you.

(*He throws them a kiss. A moment's silence. A boy calls out.*)

BOY: Goodbye, Father.

(*All the students join in.*)

ALL: Goodbye, Father.

(*A soldier gives FATHER JEAN a brutal shove out into the street. BONNET, also pushed, turns for a moment in the gateway. His eyes search for JULIEN, who takes a step forward and gives him a little wave. BONNET is gone. We stay with JULIEN standing a little in front of the others. He is staring at the empty entranceway. Over this child's face we hear an adult voice.*)

VOICE: Bonnet, Négus, and Dupré died in Auschwitz, Father Jean in the camp at Mauthausen. The school reopened its doors in October 1944. Over forty years have passed, but I will remember every second of that January morning until the day I die.

Louis Malle

b. October 30, 1932, / Thumeries, France

Filmography

DATE	TITLE	ENGLISH RELEASE TITLE
1956	*Le Monde du silence* (documentary)	*The Silent World*
1957	*Ascenseur pour l'échafaud*	*Elevator to the Gallows*
1958	*Les Amants*	*The Lovers*
1960	*Zazie dans le métro*	*Zazie*
1961	*Vie Privée*	*A Very Private Affair*
1962	*Vive le tour* (documentary)	
1963	*Feu follet*	*The Fire Within*
1964	*Bons Baisers de Bangkok* (documentary)	
1965	*Viva Maria*	
1966	*Le Voleur*	*The Thief of Paris*
1967	*Histoires extraordinaires* (one episode)	*Spirits of the Dead*
1969	*Calcutta* (documentary)	
1969	*L'Inde fantôme* (documentaries)	*Phantom India*
1970	*Le Souffle au coeur*	*Murmur of the Heart*
1972	*Humain, trop humain* (documentary)	
1973	*Place de la République* (documentary)	
1974	*Lacombe, Lucien*	
1975	*Black Moon*	

DATE	TITLE
1977	*Pretty Baby*
1980	*Atlantic City*
1981	*My Dinner with André*
1983	*Crackers*
1984	*Alamo Bay*
1985	*God's Country* (documentary)
1986	*And the Pursuit of Happiness* (documentary)
1987	*Au revoir les enfants*